What to do when your mom or dad says... "GET DRESSED!"

By
JOY BERRY

 CHILDRENS PRESS ®
CHICAGO

Children's Press
1987 School and Library Edition
ISBN 0-516-02592-9

CREDITS

Producer
  Ron Berry

Editor
  Orly Kelly

"GET DRESSED!"

Has your mother or father ever told you to . . .

Whenever you are told to get dressed, do you wonder. . .

If any of this sounds familiar to you, you are going to **love** this book.

Because it will tell you exactly how to decide what to wear every time you need to get dressed.

WEARING THE RIGHT OUTFIT

Before you decide what you are going to wear, you will need to ask yourself four questions:

1. Where will I be going?

If you will be going someplace casual (like school, a friend's house, or someplace outdoors), wear your playclothes.

If you will be going someplace more formal (like a fancy party or restaurant, a church, or the theater), wear your dressy clothes.

2. What will I be doing?

If you will be doing something that is active (like running, playing a sport, or riding a bike), wear sturdy clothes that you can move around in safely and easily.

If you will be doing something that is more reserved (like watching a performance), wear clothes that are not so casual or sturdy.

3. When will I be going?

If you are going at a time of year when it will be hot, wear something cool.

If you are going at a time of day when it will be warm, wear something cool.

4. Whom will I be with?

Wear something that you will enjoy wearing around the other person.

WEARING THE RIGHT COLORS

The colors of your skin, hair, and eyes are most important to consider in choosing what colors you are going to wear. The best way to decide what colors go best with your skin, hair, and eyes is to try on many colors to see which look best.

Colors that match your hair and eyes will almost always look good on you.

Here is a chart to help you decide which colors might look best on you.

If your coloring is:	Try to wear these colors:
Pale to pink skin/ blonde hair	Beige (if your skin is not too pale), violet, mauve, navy, blue, green, peach
Dark skin/blonde to light-brown hair	Burnt orange and rust, red, gold, bright blue, beige, olive green, brown, peach
Fair to rosy skin/red hair	Pink, violet, purple, navy, bright blue, pastel blue, white, gray, black
Dark or olive skin/red hair	Brown, apricot, beige, light brown, rust, deep brown
Fair skin/brown to black hair	Blue, white, yellow, gold, red, mauve, purple, navy, bright blue, pastel blue, gray, brown
Dark skin/brown to black hair	Bright colors, such as turquoise, bright green, raspberry, purple, pink

PALE SKIN
BLONDE HAIR

DARK SKIN
BLONDE TO LIGHT
BROWN HAIR

FAIR SKIN
RED HAIR

OLIVE SKIN
RED HAIR

FAIR SKIN
BROWN TO
BLACK HAIR

DARK SKIN
BROWN TO BLACK
HAIR.

WHAT ABOUT
ME?

19

Some colors look good with any color. These are called neutral colors.

Neutral colors include black, white, and beige. Gray, navy blue, and cordovan may also be used as neutral colors.

It's good for you to have neutral-colored accessories, such as shoes, belts, purses, and jackets.

This is because neutral accessories can be worn with anything in your wardrobe.

WEARING THE RIGHT PATTERNS

The fabrics that clothes are made of come in several different patterns.

Plain fabrics are solid colors with no designs.

Prints are fabrics with pictures and designs.

Stripes are fabrics with vertical or horizontal lines.

Checks have both vertical and horizontal lines, which are usually the same width and color.

Plaids have both vertical and horizontal lines. The lines are of different colors and widths.

Polka dots are fabrics with solid circles printed all over them.

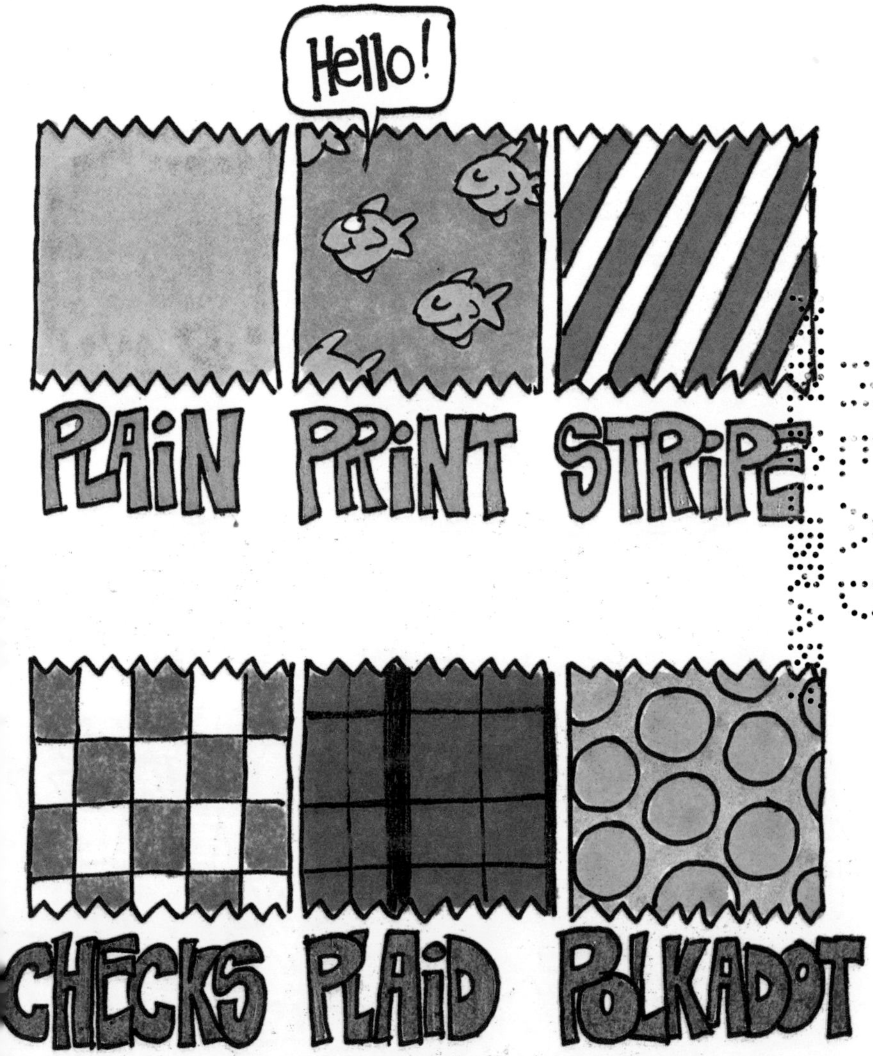
Hello!
PLAIN
PRINT
STRIPE
CHECKS
PLAID
POLKADOT

It's fun to have clothes that are different patterns. But, many patterns do not look well when worn together. Remember the following to make sure your outfits look right.

- Wear plain pants or a plain skirt if your shirt or blouse is made of a print, striped, checked, plaid, or polka-dot material.

Make sure that the color of the pants or skirt matches a color in the shirt or blouse.

- If the pattern of your skirt or pants is a print, stripe, check, plaid, or polka dot, wear a plain shirt or blouse.

THE ONLY THING THAT WOULD MATCH WOULD BE YOU AND A THREE-RING CIRCUS!

WRONG

- Make sure that the color of the shirt or blouse matches a color in the pants or skirt.

- Try not to mix prints, stripes, checks, plaids, and polka dots, because your outfit will probably look confusing.

29

WEARING THE RIGHT STYLES

The size and shape of your body are very important in choosing clothes.

If you are tall, you will probably look best in—

- plaids
- prints
- full skirts (for girls)
- soft ruffled blouses (for girls)
- pleated pants
- contrasting colors
- horizontal lines
- bulky sweaters

You might want to avoid—

- severely tailored clothes
- one-color outfits
- vertical lines

If you are short, you will probably look best in—

- single-colored outfits or coordinated outfits
- clothes with small (rather than large) details
- short vests and jackets (for girls)
- pleated skirts (for girls)
- vertical lines or stitching

You might want to avoid—

- hems that are longer than 2" below the knee (for girls)
- hems that are shorter than 2" above the knee (for girls)
- horizontal lines

If you are slender, you will probably look best in—

- the layered look
- plaids
- prints
- full skirts (for girls)
- bulky sweaters

- soft ruffled blouses (for girls)
- pleated pants
- contrasting colors
- horizontal lines

You might want to avoid—

- severely tailored clothes
- one-color outfits
- vertical lines

If you are heavy, you will probably look best in—

- darker colors
- flared skirts (for girls)
- tailored pants
- long or three-quarter length sleeves
- simple styles

You might want to avoid—

- bright colors
- large plaids
- large prints
- shiny fabrics
- extra frills (for girls)

- "way-out" styles
- pleated skirts (for girls)
- pleated pants
- clothes that fit tightly or loosely

WEARING THE RIGHT
WEIGHT OF CLOTHING

Some fabrics, such as wool, corduroy, felt, and quilted fabrics, are heavy. Clothes made of heavy fabrics should be worn in the fall and winter because they keep you warm.

Other fabrics, such as cotton, polyester, rayon, and nylon are light. Clothes made of lightweight fabrics should be worn in the spring and summer because they will let you be cool.

WEARING THE RIGHT CUT OF CLOTHING

Some clothes are designed to cover your whole body so that you will not get cold. Shirts and blouses with high necks and long sleeves should be worn in the fall and winter because they keep you warm. The same is true of long skirts and pants.

Clothes that do not cover very much of your body allow you to be cooler. Low-necked, short-sleeved, or sleeveless shirts and blouses should be worn in the spring and summer. The same is true for short pants.

WEARING CLOTHES THAT FIT

To look your very best, it is important that your clothes fit you properly.

The following describes a good fit for girls:

1. Long sleeves should not be too short or too long. When your arm is hanging down, your sleeve should end where your wrist and hand are joined.
2. Your shoulder seam should not hang off your shoulder. It should be at the top of your shoulder where the curve begins.
3. The waistline of your pants and skirts should fit you comfortably and not be too tight or too loose.
4. The hem of your sweater and jacket should be at waist level, at the bottom of the buttocks, or somewhere in between.
5. The hem of your pants should almost touch the top of your shoes.
6. The hem of your skirts and dresses should be between 2" above and 2" below your knees.
7. The hem of your long coat should be 2" or 3" longer than the hem of your skirt or dress.
8. You should never wear clothing that is too loose or too tight.

43

The following describes a good fit for boys:

1. Long sleeves should not be too short or too long. When your arm is hanging down, your sleeve should end where your wrist and hand are joined.
2. Your shoulder seam should not hang off your shoulder. It should be at the top of your shoulder where the curve begins.
3. The waistline of your pants should fit you comfortably and not be too tight or too loose.
4. The hem of your sweater and jacket should be at waist level, at the bottom of the buttocks, or somewhere in between.

When you "dress up":
   5. Your shirt collar should be out and lying flat.
   6. Your shirttail should be tucked in.
   7. Your coat collar should hug your neck at the back and sides.
   8. One-half inch of your shirt should show above the collar of your jacket.
   9. One-half inch of your shirt sleeve should show below your jacket sleeve when your arm is hanging down.
10. If you wear a two-button jacket, the bottom button should be at belt level.
11. If you wear a three-button jacket, the middle button should be at belt level.

Here is another picture of a girl
who is not dressed properly.

Here is another picture of a boy who is not dressed properly.

THE END of not knowing what to wear.